Ọ̀LỌ́BÙN

MATRIARCH OF ONDO, MOTHER OF LEGACY

Another book by Tomi Falade

Ọ̀LỌ́BÙN

MATRIARCH OF ONDO, MOTHER OF LEGACY

TOMI FALADE

KIYESOLA MEDIA
Ojodu, Ikeja, Lagos, Nigeria

First published in Nigeria in 2024 by Kiyesola Media

A catalogue for this book is available from the National Library, Nigeria

ISBN 978-978-787-214-7

Printed and Bound in Nigeria by Print Doctor Africa

Photography by @akinjidephotography
Cover Design by @TheRealAdeoba

To find out more about the author and her books, please visit tomifalade.com.

DEDICATION

Dedicated to God,

the creator of all things.

&

My father,

Thomas Olajide Falade –

from whose lips I first heard the words:

Ilẹ Oluji.

AUTHOR'S NOTE

Olobun's story is an integral part of the people of Ondo's history. However, beneath her significance to the Ondo Kingdom lies a beginning I've attempted to document.

I have always been surrounded by strong women, especially my mother. Against the odds, she transforms into whatever role I require in my life - a defender, a financier, an adviser, a manager, an editor, a critic, or simply a friend. She is the foundation for my profound connection to Olobun's story. Olobun, like my mother, adapted to fulfill the needs of history. Yet, with the passage of centuries, historical details fade, risking distortion. This work is my endeavour to secure her history, anchoring it with my skills as a writer.

It is noteworthy that I have taken creative liberties with the original story for the sake of artistic beauty. Some parts of this work are entirely fictional, albeit mythical. Nevertheless, the core of the story remains true to the history of the esteemed Ondo Kingdom, and these parts can be validated by custodians of the Ekimogun lore.

A child on an unplanned journey finds it difficult to predict the end of that journey, she can only hope. When I began writing this book, I lacked a clear objective or endpoint. All I knew was that I needed to tell a story.

14 years after I started writing this, my efforts have yielded better fruit beyond my wildest expectations. I owe these people thanks:

Grace Modupe Oluwatoyin Falade, my mother whose room full of books sparked my love for the written word. My birthdays were magical because of the many storybooks she bought me. From young authors to established ones she bought them, and I devoured them just as easily. May God bless and keep you.

Mr Doyin Owobamirin, the lecturer at Olabisi Onabanjo University who recognised my love for theatre and facilitated invaluable contacts at the Ondo Cultural Centre for my research. I remain profoundly grateful for your assistance.

Funmilayo, Motunlayo, and Ayoyinka, my beautiful sisters who endured the relentless clacking of my keyboard and my erratic schedules, I am thankful for the privilege of sharing my life with you. This is just the beginning.

The Jide-Fadiya family, my second family, thank you for your unwavering support and for embracing this project like a newborn baby.

My media family, I am grateful for the invaluable lessons.

To the management and staff of INDEPENDENT Newspapers, particularly Mr Steve Omanufeme, the MD, and Mr. Yemi Adebisi, my editor, thank you for allowing me to be truly independent.

I must particularly mention some others whose impact on my growth helped bring this to life.

Rotimi Ige, I am grateful for the memories. Thank you for your genuine friendship. Gbenga Bada, for sharing your wisdom and abilities, I am indebted. Mrs. Tope Lawanson, my 'ride or die,' I cherish the gift of you. Olamide Arowosegbe, for standing by me always, thank you.

Gbenga Adeyinka D 1st, with his ever-ready yes; Temiyemi Akintomide, my little darling; Dolapo Ebadan - my third-eyed confidante; Yetunde Ojelade;

Testimony 'Eri' Adebisi, the hardest working 'Gen Z' I know; Tofarati Ige and the rest of the media geng; Ola Awakan; Oladele Oladipo; and Mr. Kayode Alfred, my perpetual journalism teacher - you are all beautiful souls.

Mr. Seun Oloketuyi, you are an exceptional friend, one that is indispensable. I am grateful for all you do and represent.

Thank you all.

Tomi Falade

ACT ONE

SCENE I

(A village setting. The wind howls, announcing the arrival of the rains. Women are seen with backs bent over uncooperative fires. There is no man in immediate sight. The clouds are heavy with the unceasing floods that have besieged the land for months.)

ADUKE: Why won't you light? There's barely enough time to make dinner before the arrival of the rain, yet you stupid wood has refused to embrace the fire. Or did I stack it wrong? Olódùmarè, why this hardship? To think Fagboro has said that a big gift is coming that would pave the way for our happiness this year. Yet, ten months have gone by and it's been from one calamity to another. Light! You foolish wood, light!

(As she soliloquises, her husband, Folaranmi, walks in, hoe in hand, evidently returning from the farm.)

FOLA: E kuule o!

ADUKE: My lord, welcome. I hope all is well. You are home earlier than usual? And I've just begun preparations for dinner.

FOLA: We saw the approach of the storm and many at the farms thought it best that the storm meets us indoors where it is safe. After all, it is better to be alive and wretched than dead and prosperous.

ADUKE: But my husband, you are the only man here. Other men are not home yet. Was the decision yours only? Or were you the only one who saw the coming storm?

FOLA: Silence, woman! Are you questioning my words, or what are you on about? You prattle all day like a parrot cursed by the gods instead of cooking a decent meal for your deserving, hardworking husband. You haven't even lit the firewood, something your child should be doing by now if not that Olódùmarè has locked your womb for fear that you would kill your offspring with your wild chatter.

ADUKE: Ahn ahn! Did I offend you before you left for the farm? *(Quietly)* This one that you are foaming at the mouth like a rabid dog.

FOLA: Am I the one you are talking to? May Sopona...

ADUKE: Olowo ori mi, I'm sorry. It's just that you are being unnecessarily cruel.

FOLA: Let me just go inside and rest. I guess I'm a little tired. *(Goes into the house grumbling about women.)*

ADUKE: Tired indeed. You'd better confess what you have been doing *(Hisses. The wind howls and blows violently).* Ehn! I'd better go inside and leave this fire. We will drink gaari with the remnant of yesterday's fish.

(Exits)

SCENE II

(Inside the house is brightly lit by lanterns. Fola and his wife can be seen eating when they hear a knock at the door.)

ADUKE: Who can it be at this time when all sane men have kept to the comfort of their homes? Even the insane have sought the shelter of Weretedo's (the healer of all insanity) abode. Stray goats have learned not to wander far for fear of being carried away by the storm, yet here comes a knock at our door. *(Turns to her husband)* Are you expecting someone?

FOLA: Is that not what you should have done first before rendering your incessant incantations like a mad woman? Anyway, Fagboro said he'd call on us tonight on the issue of your childlessness. *(Moving to open the door)* Abi is that not important?

ADUKE: It is o, my lord. It is.

(Enter Fagboro chanting a series of incantations and rendering a praise chant of twins to the bewilderment of the couple.)

FOLA: Baba, you are welcome.

ADUKE: Have a seat.

(They offer him a seat which he takes and remains silent until he has eaten a part of their fish and become comfortable.)

FAGBORO: Dear ones, I bear good tidings from Olódùmarè who has this year granted all good things in doubles.

FOLA: Baba, you have spoken well. *(Aduke tries to contradict what her husband has said, but he steps on her feet and presses on)* What is the message?

FAGBORO: *(Facing Aduke)* Tonight, when the storm is at its fiercest, go to the place where there are yam stalks, at the entrance of our village and pour out your heart. Say everything you have to say, for you own the ears of the gods tonight. After that, slowly make your way back home. Whatever you find on your way back, bring to my house at the crack of dawn before anyone is up and about.

ADUKE: But Baba, what will I find? If I take something that belongs to someone else, you know I will be flogged for stealing. This abstract message you are...

FOLA: *(Silences her)* Thank you, Baba. She'll do as you have instructed.

(With that, Fagboro rises to leave and reminds Aduke to walk home slowly so she can find what needs to be found)

FOLA: Make sure you say everything o, because that is when you'll start blabbing like a baboon!

ADUKE: Baale mi! You sent a gossip to deliver a message and you are insisting that she delivers the message well. Who will say more than you have instructed if not the gossip?

FOLA: My point exactly. Remember to speak coherently and ask for precise things.

ADUKE: I've heard you.

SCENE III

(The wind is fierce and Aduke can be seen with wet clothes struggling against the wind to get to her destination. At a point, she looks undecided as she looks in the homeward direction, wondering whether to go back home and abandon her mission. However, the wind gives her no choice as it changes directions and sweeps her headlong towards her destination).

ADUKE: Olódùmarè, why have you chosen to make me barren? Why has my body unlike other women refused to yield the crimson flow of womanhood? When will my aging body feel the vibrations of childbearing? When will my body give life to another? Olódùmarè, I petition you tonight to heed my cry and hear the voice of my suffering. May my hands not remain bare in the presence of other mothers. May my offspring walk this very soil on which I kneel. May my living not be in vain. Give me a child! And I will return to give thanks. Make me a mother, and I promise not to fail in that duty.

(At this point, she retreats and heads back home. A few meters into her journey home, she begins to hear soft mewling and she follows the sound to a shack on the border of the road to the stream. There, she finds a baby girl wrapped in a rich aso-oke with costly beads known as iyun in a basket. The

baby has two long tribal marks on either side of her cheeks. Aduke immediately picks up the basket and runs home to her husband.)

SCENE IV

(It is the crack of dawn. Fola and his wife, Aduke, can be seen making their way quietly to Fagboro's house. Aduke is carrying a bundle, evidently the baby, but they make as little noise as possible. They get to Fagboro's house and knock. The door is opened by Fagboro himself and he shuts the door immediately after them.)

FAGBORO: What happened? What did you find? What is that in your hands?

FOLA: Baba, this is what she found and brought home.

FAGBORO: *(Peeps into the bundle and retreats hastily, turning from them)* Eh! Olódùmarè, these people have gone and added to their catalogue of problems. *(Turns to them)* Are you mad?

COUPLE: Ahn ahn!

FAGBORO: Yes! Or is it not only people of the insane breed that would do what you have done? I sent you on a mission and told you to only bring back what Olódùmarè gives you as a sign that he has heard your cry, and you bring me a cursed child.

FOLA: But Baba, how do you know she's cursed?

ADUKE: You have not even touched her yet...

FAGBORO: Touch, you say? My generation will not bless me if I do that. Have you ever seen a child so marked in these parts? Anyway, that is by the way. I need to consult *Ifá* to know what to do next. *(Points them to the floor)* Sit down and keep that cursed child away from my sight so I can consult in peace.

ADUKE: *(Hisses and sits reluctantly)* Instead of admitting his own mistake, he is blaming us. Why didn't he tell me last night when he tottered like a chicken from our house with half the fish that should have been our dinner?

FOLA: You had better keep your mouth shut or I'll do it for you. Have you no respect for the old man?

ADUKE: My lord, it is just that...

FAGBORO: *(Cuts in)* What manner of madness plagues you people? Will you let me consult *Ifá* in peace or should I just send you away with your cursed baby?

FOLA: Baba, we are sorry. It won't happen again *(stepping on Aduke's toes)*. Abi will it?

ADUKE: No o, Baba! It won't.

(He casts a scathing look at them and continues his consultation. He casts his opele many times, his expression going puzzled)

FAGBORO: It appears that *Ifá* does not wish to reveal the true nature of things to me. But from what I can see here, the girl is a twin, and she has a great destiny. Both are to be her guardian for the time being until that appointed time when she will fulfil her purpose on earth. In doing this, *Ifá* says you will get your own reward.

(The couple looks at Fagboro in amazement.)

FAGBORO: Ehn, say something. Abi why have you suddenly grown silent like people cursed with dumbness? A while ago, it took all of my willpower to restrain myself from throwing you out because of your persistent chatter; now, when I actually need you to talk, your tongues have suddenly grown limp.

FOLA: *(Regaining composure)* Sorry, Baba. Your words petrified us.

FAGBORO: Go and be petrified in your house. (*Rethinks*) There was one thing *Ifá* was clear about though. She must be protected and preserved. For security reasons, I think it would be expedient for you to leave this village for a while to avoid prying eyes and idle talk concerning the child. I suggest you take her into the forest, far away from people. Those marks on her face are strange enough.

ADUKE: We have heard you, Baba. But how long are we to stay away because...

FAGBORO: *(Cuts in)* You can now leave my house!

ADUKE: Baba, I...

FAGBORO: *(Cuts in again)* Go! Before you awaken the entire village with your ranting.

FOLA: What do we do with the beads?

FAGBORO: What beads? You spoke of no beads.

ADUKE: Well, you gave us no chance. I found some *iyun* beside the *aso-oke* she was wrapped in.

FAGBORO: *(Thoughtfully)* Well, since we aren't privy to the mystery surrounding her birth, I suggest you keep the beads. Now, go! May Olódùmarè protect you.

COUPLE: Ase!

(Exits)

ACT TWO

Scene I

(17 years later, the couple and their two daughters, Iyunola, with her noticeable tribal marks, and Omowamiri, move back to their homeland. Two women pass them on their way to the stream and begin to comment on their arrival.)

FADEKE: Bimpe, are you sure you don't remember Folaranmi and his wife, Aduke, anymore?

OLABIMPE: Fadeke, I have told you I don't remember them. Now, let me be and leave other people's matters that don't concern us.

FADEKE: Ahn ahn! You mean you don't remember Aduke, the childless one who chatters all day like...

OLABIMPE: Like you!

FADEKE: Ehn?

OLABIMPE: Ehn! Like you. Now that you've reminded me of her identity, I seem to notice that she left a replacement of herself in you when she left town, seeing as she is now as quiet as a dove and you as talkative as a parrot.

FADEKE: I don't like these insults that seem to be in heavy supply from you today.

OLABIMPE: Neither do I like the parrot in you. But I obviously have to contend with it, don't I?

FADEKE: How come you are the only one that does not enjoy my company? Better humans than you crave my company day after day, and here you are treating me like a pest.

OLABIMPE: Then go to those better people. Deke. Go!

FADEKE: Okay, I'm sorry. I didn't mean it that way. Don't chase me away, please Olabimpe.

OLABIMPE: Look, let's just go.

FADEKE: But Aduke is really looking better now, especially in the company of those two young girls. They must be her daughters. Or what do you think?

OLABIMPE: 'Deke, must you talk? Can't you just keep quiet for once in your life?

FADEKE: Okay o!

(Exits)

SCENE II

(Fola can be seen sharpening his matchet, while Aduke and the girls attend to food matters.)

ADUKE: My lord, it feels good to be back in our home, amongst our own people.

FOLA: Yes o! But peace seems to be far from the land. The people are too restive to pass for a happy community. I think it's because the land still has no king or royal custodian. There's no sense of belonging yet, and it seems Oyo has forgotten about this place.

ADUKE: *(Sitting beside her husband)* My lord, I suggest we go to Fagboro and see him as soon as possible. After all, that's the reason we are back home.

FOLA: Yes, you are right. We'll go at dusk because I do not want the whole village to see us at Fagboro's house so soon after our return. You know how well our people's tongues do justice to secrets.

ADUKE: Yes, my lord. *(Rising)* Let me go and continue with dinner.

SCENE III

(Late at night, Aduke and Fola arrive at Fagboro's hut with Iyunola and Omowamiri in tow.)

FAGBORO: Ha! Folaranmiiiiiiii, you are welcome. How was your journey?

FOLA: Ha! Baba, we thank Olódùmarè. He has really blessed us.

FAGBORO: *(Looking at Iyunola).* And I think this is the child?

FOLA: Yes, this is Iyunola, our daughter, and the reason we are back home after so many years.

FAGBORO: All right. Sit down, all of you. Aduke, I see age has tempered the potency of your tongue.

ADUKE: *(Laughing and sitting).* Baba, it is good to see you, too.

FAGBORO: So, tell me, Fola, what is the problem? Why have you chosen to visit me in the cloak of darkness?

FOLA: It all started when Iyunola was eleven. She began to hear the voice of someone, Orayan, who claims she is his descendant.

FAGBORO: What!

FOLA: Yes! Surprisingly, none of us hears the voice; she says he keeps telling her that her name is ***Olobun***, and that she is a princess.

FAGBORO: *(Brings out his opele and begins panegyrics)* I'm the blind one. You are the one who sees it all. Unravel the mystery to us. *(Faces Iyun)* My daughter, in these revelations or episodes you've been having, has there been any other thing that has been revealed to you?

IYUNOLA: Yes, Baba. The voice keeps telling me to go to Ile Oluji.

ALL: Ile Oluji?

IYUNOLA: Yes. I didn't tell my parents because I have never heard of Ile Oluji.

FOLA: That is because the village you speak of is only a myth. There have been many stories in times past, but no one can confirm it. Many years after you were found, there were tales that there was a village, a small settlement that Olu, favourite wife of Alaafin Oluaso of Oyo, descendant of Oranyan, died in. It was then named after her 'the land where Olu slept and did not wake'. She was claimed by many to have been murdered in her sleep, but no one has found the mythical village to date.

ADUKE: It's just a figment of people's imaginations, stories concocted to...

FAGBORO: *(Cuts in)* Stories yes, but that doesn't make it a lie. The legend is that only an Alaafin descendant by right would locate the place and then rule over it and the surrounding villages. It is actually not too far from her, but no one has ever been able to locate it.

IYUNOLA: Baba mi, perhaps if we journey to Oyo and seek an audience with Alaafin himself, we will find a solution to my problem. It is getting harder to be alone, let alone sleep. The voice haunts me day and night now.

FOLA: *(Laughs long and hard).* Look at this child; you want to seek an audience with Alaafin, *Alase Ekeji Orisa, Alaafin*, second in command to the gods, owner of the palace. You must be joking.

(Fagboro ignores them and consults the oracle)

FOLA: *(Faces Fagboro)* Baba, we have no connection to Alaafin whatsoever. His palace is far away in Oyo, and our problems are here with us. It gets bigger by the day, especially when we try our best to ignore it.

FAGBORO: Enough of your chattering. I see you have taken over from your wife. Go home and prepare for another journey. From what I have seen, the girl will find her path. Both of you are her guides chosen by destiny to help her with her search. Whenever she feels ready to leave the village you must go with her because if she doesn't find what she is looking for, we will all know no peace. That is the message.

IYUNOLA: But Baba, what am I supposed to be looking for? Is it Ile Oluji or peace for us?

FAGBORO: I think it is all the same thing. In finding Ile Oluji, we all find peace.

ADUKE: Baba, we came to you with one problem you are adding more to it. Where do we begin our search? How?

FAGBORO: Stop battering me with your questions. Olódùmarè himself knows I have not seen more than I have told you. This is a peculiar case and we must tread with caution. Iyunola's journey has just started, but it will be a great one. Always remember that. The greatest people are those who have yet to reach their destination. Help her reach her destination. She has a very big purpose.

FOLA: Okay, Baba. We have heard you, and we'll do our best to ensure that she gets to her destination.

SCENE IV

(It is the middle of the night, and Iyunola can be heard screaming. Her parents rush in to check on her)

ADUKE: Iyun, is he back? Why are you screaming? You scared us.

IYUNOLA: Baba Oranyan came again, and he showed me a place. He said I should go east of this place, and that I'll find it.

FOLA: Then journey we shall. This is the third time you have had this particular dream, and only Olódùmarè knows the consequences of not heeding. We leave at dawn. Aduke, wake Omowamiri and start packing. Pack only the necessary things, mostly food. One day, we will return to this land and find peace.

ADUKE: And if we never do?

FOLA: Then what would be the use of taking so many things with us? Just the necessities. The lighter we travel, the faster we are.

ADUKE: All right, my lord.

ACT THREE

SCENE I

(Fola and his family can be seen going through the forest walking and dragging a tired Wamiri)

FOLA: Wamiri, will you stop being so lazy? Do you think the rest of us are not tired? You are just compounding our problems. Can't you see that it is important we move as fast as possible? We should have left you at home alone, so you understand the gravity of the whole situation.

ADUKE: My lord, don't be too hard on her. We have been on this road for two days now.

IYUN: Wamiri, don't mind father. We will soon be at the place. Okay? Then you can rest as much as you want. Right now, I need you to be strong. Please, for my sake. I even promise to share my dinner with you.

WAMIRI: Really? In that case I'm strong as an ox!

ADUKE: *(To Fola)* Look at her rejoicing. If only she knew dinner tonight is the rest of the roasted esuru we ate this morning. She hates esuru.

FOLA: At least, she's back on her feet and walking again. You'd better let her dream of a sumptuous meal than cut her expectations short. Keep the information about the dinner to yourself till it is necessary. That way, we can cover better distance before nightfall. (*To Iyun*) Iyun my daughter, always the optimist.

IYUN: Thanks for the compliment father. Baba Oranyan told me last night that I should always learn to look on the bright side of things. That way, I can always give my people hope.

ADUKE: Who exactly are these people you want to give hope to?

WAMIRI: Her subjects, of course.

COUPLE: Subjects?

IYUN: Oh! Didn't I tell you?

FOLA: No, you didn't.

ADUKE: What exactly didn't you tell us?

IYUN: That my eventual destination is a land where the people await their monarch. I am to become their ruler. That is why we need to make haste so that I do not lose my birthright.

FOLA: Has the lack of food and sleep driven you mad? Since when has it become your purpose or destiny to go around usurping kings and dominating kingdoms? Oh! You want to wake the sleeping mad dog. You forget, Iyun, that he who swallows a pestle does so at his peril and discomfort. When a chicken decides to make the rope its perch, then both the chicken and the rope will know no peace. You want to stir up a real hornet's nest. You...

IYUN: (*Cuts in angrily*) Enough, Baba mi! I'm only trying to claim what is rightfully mine. Besides, there's no king to usurp, not even a regent. Just an empty throne waiting for its royal custodian.

FOLA: You have forgotten, my dear daughter that only one with royal blood can be a monarch in any kingdom under the Oyo Empire. Such a king must be endorsed by the Alaafin himself and gifted with a beaded crown as a sign of his kingship. As it is, we are only as royal as you are a man.

IYUN: To start with, if Baba Oranyan is really my ancestor, then it means I have royal blood flowing through my veins. I was given these tribal marks so that whenever I return, my claim would not be questioned. My gender will also not be an issue since I am not trying to usurp the Alaafin. You need to trust me. Remember Baba Fagboro said you should guide and help me.

FOLA: That is what I'm trying to do, my dear. Abi Aduke? *(Aduke remains silent)* Woman, say something or have you suddenly misplaced your tongue?

ADUKE: What do you want me to say? Fagboro said we must go with her wherever she decides to go, now you are protesting. Look, if she says she is going to usurp Alaafin himself we must follow her.

WAMIRI: Iyun, are you really going to take over Alaafin's throne?

IYUN: (Laughs) No, Wamiri.

FOLA: I have heard you, Aduke. Just don't say I didn't warn you. Well, Iyun, which way now?

IYUN: East, always east. We should be there by morning.

SCENE II

(The family can be seen approaching an entrance guarded by two men. The guards look shocked to see them approach)

IJA: Who are these ones approaching? Humans or spirits?

ABEO: Well, Ija, judging from their tired steps and dirty clothes, I would say humans, humans who have spent too much time in the forest.

IJA: Abeo, as usual, you seem to be missing the point of my question. What I meant was that no one has come to this place in many years. Now, these strange people suddenly appear. It is only expedient that we question their identity. This place, after all, cannot be located by anyone.

ABEO: As usual, Ija, you too have missed the point of my answer. What I meant is that they are human beings who have journeyed far to get here. And to correct your obviously failing memory, the caveat does not say it cannot be located by anyone, there was an exception; only an offspring of Alaafin.

IJA: And what helped you conclude that they are related to Alaafin? Their radiant attire or their heralding entourage?

ABEO: They found Ile Oluji, didn't they?

IJA: Where then is their royal retinue? Surely, you don't think Alaafin would send any of his kin forth with no royal emblem and retinue?

ABEO: That I do not know. But since we are both standing here, I trust your ears would come out of retirement long enough to hear what they have to say.

IJA: Is it well with your father? Do you realise that I'm old enough...?

ABEO: Here they come, so do away with your bad manners and I can lend you some good manners.

IJA: I will...

FOLA: Greetings to the people of this land.

ABEO: Greetings to you, stranger. Where are you from?

FOLA: From a land not too far from here called Idi-Edo.

IJA: And your business here?

FOLA: Well, we ehn...

IYUN: Who is in charge here?

ABEO: The one who neither sleeps nor slumbers.

IYUN: Meaning there is no earthly monarch here?

IJA: Well, we, erm... it was. I am...

IYUN: Speak coherently, please. Or has the lack of fit human company dulled your brain?

FOLA: Iyun, do not speak to your elders like that.

IYUN: Father, you don't understand. We don't have any more time. Baba Oranyan told me last night that the Alaafin is about to order an *Asoju Oba* (a prince with no crown - regent) to come and rule this land. That cannot happen because if it does, I'll lose my birthright forever. He must think I'm dead.

FOLA: Just be gentle with them.

IYUN: Mother, please where are the beads?

ADUKE: What beads?

IYUN: The ones I'm named after. I need to show it to them so they can confirm my identity.

(Aduke rummages around in their luggage and eventually produces them)

ADUKE: Here they are. Thanks to Olódùmarè I brought them along.

IYUN: *(Turns to the two guards)* I am Olobun, also named Olu, twin sister to Oluade, daughter of Alaafin Oluaso and Olori Olu. I am a descendant of Oranyan, the first Alaafin of Oyo. You do recognise the marks on my face, don't you?

(The duo fall on their knees to pay obeisance.)

ABEO: You are welcome, princess. Long, have we awaited your return.

IYUN: Well, I'm glad I was eventually expected.

IJA: And who are your companions, Olobun, if we may ask?

ADUKE: Her name is Iyun, and we are her parents.

IJA: But that is impossible. Before our very own eyes, her mother died, and we all know that Alaafin is her father.

ABEO: Ija, why do you always talk like a retarded fellow. Even before our dear monarch, you can't pretend to apply wisdom to your words. No censoring at all, just pure unadulterated stupidity. We knew her as a baby and she's all grown now. Who did you think raised her? Monkeys? Of course, she has parents. They do not have to be her biological parents to be her parents.

FOLA: Thank you jare, my friend. We understand she's your monarch, but she's our daughter, too.

WAMIRI: Iyun, remember you promised I could rest when we arrived. Have we arrived? Besides, we didn't have breakfast this morning, so I'm hungry, too.

ADUKE: Can't you see we are sorting things out?

FOLA: Don't worry, you'll eat soon, my dear. Could we please get some shade maybe under a tree? My family is tired and so am I.

IJA: Ha! We can provide better accommodation than the shade of a tree.

ABEO: Accommodation befitting the parents of our queen.

IYUN: Father, we leave for Oyo tomorrow.

ALL: Tomorrow?

IYUN: Yes, I need to see Alaafin before he gifts away my heritage. Tomorrow, we go west to Oyo.

FOLA: Then we will go with you.

ACT FOUR

SCENE I

(The Alaafin of Oyo's palace is in an uproar.)

SAMU: Kabiyesi, do not make this mistake. This is someone's heritage we are disputing. Why the sudden rush anyway?

BASHORUN: Rush you say, Samu? Rush! You call the last fifteen years of waiting a rush? Obade is a legitimate prince of Oyo and long has he been without a crown to make him the king he should be. Obade! That is the name of a king.

IYALOJA: It is only the name of a king when you stand to gain from his being crowned, abi Bashorun? We all know that Obade has promised to marry your old maid of a daughter should you ensure the successful transfer of the twins' kingdom to him. The news is being peddled around Oja Oba already.

SAMU: Of course, Bashorun wouldn't be against the transfer of another's birthright if it means his daughter' sagging breasts get to be hidden in a king's royal harem.

AGBAAKIN: Ha, Samu! Do not let your mouth get you in trouble. I'm sure Bashorun's intentions are quite noble.

ALAPINI: Leave him. Let him run his mouth like one who feasted on a breakfast of okra and *ewura* yam. I wouldn't blame him anyway; it is common knowledge that his wife is a Tapa slave. How then will he appreciate the honour of marrying a daughter from our Bashorun's prestigious family?

SAMU: Don't you dare insult my wife or else...

BASHORUN: Or else what? Oh, now the shoe is on the other foot and you understand how it feels.

IYALOJA: What shoe? Whose foot? Samu was only pointing out the truth of the situation.

BASHORUN: And Alapini reciprocated in kind!

AGBAAKIN: Look chiefs, we need to stop bickering like market women haggling over goods. We are supposed to be the king's eyes and ears in the kingdom, but it seems we only have eyes and ears for what is going on inside one another's soup pots. The matter for which we convened has not been settled and you are flying at each other's throats. Bashorun, when a child is behaving like a child, must the elder follow suit?

SAMU: Agbaakin!

IYALOJA: Is all well with you upstairs? Who is the child here?

ALAAFIN: Enough!

ALL: Kabiyesi ooo!

ALAAFIN: Do not Kabiyesi me! What a disgrace you lot are! What manner of council is this? Your job is to counsel the king, yet you bicker like chickens over a grain of corn. The decision to consider gifting the twins' heritage was not one I took on a whim. It is born out of the need to keep the kingdom whole. *(Alaafin begins to pace)* Oyo cannot appear weak. It didn't happen with my fathers, and it won't start with me. We are surrounded by enemies and leaving our lands without a royal custodian is like an invitation to those Nupe bastards. It is the ultimate sign of weakness.

I loved Olu dearly. I loved her so much that I broke tradition for her when the birth of the twins almost broke her. You all know it's a taboo to bear twins in

Oyo. But how could I put the children of my beloved, my *aayo*, through such pain? I have many children, but these ones were too special. You were all present when Ifá provided an alternative measure to their death.

AGBA: Yes, Kabiyesi. We were all present when Ifá said they should be sent away from main Oyo to a land where yam sprouted called Idi-Edo by the settlers.

ALAAFIN: And that I did! But how was I to know that evil would not leave them? When Ija, the hunter, brought news that Oluade, my boy, was killed at Epe before the royal retinue could escape, I thought Olódùmarè had at least spared Olobun. But since then, no one has set eyes on her. Many of you do not know this, but for the two years I was away from Oyo, I was visiting Olu in the land they now call Ile Oluji where my beloved wife died.

ALL: What!

ALAAFIN: Yes! She told me that she entrusted the child to her servant while the battle raged hot. But even though *Ifá* says the child lives, no one has seen her. The marks I gave her and her brother should have made her stand out, but all of the scouts I sent from Ile Oluji returned to Oyo with no news. It's been 17 long years with no news and I need some closure. Olu is dead and I have mourned her, but now that chapter needs to end.

BASHORUN: Kabiyesi, if I may. Have you forgotten that even if Olobun is alive, it is a taboo for her to return to Oyo? She's after all still a twin child. *Ese omo* (a taboo child).

ALAAFIN: Are you questioning me? Our laws on the killing of twins have brought me so much misery. From today, that law no longer exists! I, Alaafin Oluaso, abolish the killing of twins from this day. I will no longer allow the killing of children in my domain.

BASHORUN: What!

SAMU: Kabiyesi, are you sure of your decision?

ALAAFIN: Did I stutter when I was talking? Alaafin Oranyan visited me last night and we spoke at length.

ALAPINI: I beg your pardon, Kabiyesi, but Alaafin Oranyan is dead. He died a long time ago.

ALAAFIN: *(Laughs)* Kings do not die; they remain in the vicinity of the palace to guide the reigning king, especially when the reigning king's cabinet is filled with drooling old fools.

AGBA: Ha, Kabiyesi! We are only trying to help.

SAMU: Kabiyesi, may you live long. What did Alaafin Oranyan say?

ALAAFIN: Well, there was a lot he did not say. He only said the killing of innocent children must stop during my reign. I thought long and hard about it and realised that the only children killed in Oyo are twins. From this day, it is an offence punishable by death for anyone to kill twins.

ALL: Kabiyesi oo!

ALAAFIN: That said, I believe that I have denied the people of Idi-Edo a monarch long enough. I cannot continue to watch them live without a sovereign. It leaves them open to enemies of Oyo and all sorts of evils. That land is a part of our territory and Oyo must take charge of protecting them by providing them a ruler. Obade will go there in a fortnight and take charge of the kingdom. *(Alaafin leaves)*

ALL: Kabiyesi oo!

(The royal drums announce the presence of Olori Olu, the king's dead wife. Kabiyesi returns looking perplexed)

ALAAFIN: Listen to the drums. What do they say?

SAMU: Kabiyesi, it seems the drums are announcing the presence of Olori Olu.

ALAAFIN: Have the drummers lost their wits? What madness has besieged them that they have begun to see ghosts? *(Turns to the chiefs)* Move! Find out what is happening and stop acting like idiots petrified by Sopona. Stop that crazy herald from continuing this beat of madness!

(Samu goes out and returns in panic)

SAMU: Kabiyesi, the drummers are not mad. I saw her with my own two eyes.

IYALOJA: What are you saying?

SAMU: Kabiyesi, a strange thing has come into town! It is Olu indeed.

ALAAFIN: Samu, it cannot be Olu! I would know if she were still alive. I felt her presence leave me even before I received news of her death. Could it be that...?

(A knowing look crosses Samu's face as recognition dawns on him)

SAMU: Come to think of it, Kabiyesi, the person I saw looked too young. My eyes saw Olu, but I'm not so sure anymore.

(Pandemonium breaks out. The chiefs are frantic. Iyaloja and Samu run back to investigate.)

ALAAFIN: Bashorun, Agbaakin, go with them and see what the drummers are talking about.

BASHORUN: Kabiyesi, in all my years on earth, I have never heard of a ghost returning to its homeland. An *akudaya* only goes to a new land to start a new life. I believe this ghost has come to destroy Oyo. We should kill it before it enters the palace.

(Iyaloja runs back in with Samu in tow.)

ALAAFIN: Did you see Olu?

IYALOJA: Kabiyesi, she looked to me to be younger than she was when she left, and she has fading facial marks. I-I-I think it is...

ALAPINI: Iyaloja, why are you stammering like a parrot with hot coals in its mouth? Have you not heard of an *akudaya* becoming younger when they reincarnate? We need to chase this ghost away so our king does not set eyes on this evil!

(Another set of arguments break out among the chiefs.)

ALAAFIN: Enough of this! Show her in and let us get to the bottom of the matter.

(Samu goes out and the rest of the chiefs become uneasy. He returns with Olobun who is dressed in royal attire. Alaafin looks frozen for a minute, but then he relaxes and smiles as

recognition dawns on him. Olobun and her retinue traditionally pay obeisance.)

ALAAFIN: Welcome home, my daughter. Long have I awaited your return.

IYUN: *(Curtsying)* Alaafin, it is good to finally be here.

IYALOJA: I knew it couldn't be Olu but her...

ALAPINI: Enough Iyaloja. Enough of this ghostly charade! Olori Olu is dead and if the rest of you can't see that, then I refuse to stay in the same room with this ghost. *(Stands)*

SAMU: Alapini, how dare you imply the girl is a ghost. She may look like Olu, but she is not Olu. You heard her call Kabiyesi father and you still cannot guess her identity?

ALAPINI: I refuse to stay in the same room with a ghost. Kabiyesi oo! *(He exits)*

CHIEFS: Alapini! Alapini!

ALAAFIN: Leave him. I have other pressing matters I must attend to. Olobun, these guards I remember, but the man and woman who accompany you, I do not know.

IYUN: They are my parents. They found me after I was abandoned.

ALAAFIN: Abandoned?

BASHORUN: Erm, Kabiyesi. I'm sure it is a long story. Perhaps Olobun should rest, after which she can tell her story.

ALAAFIN: *(To Fola and Aduke)* Good people, you are welcome to my palace. Eat and rest. Tomorrow, I will hear your story.

ALL: Kabiyesi ooo!

SCENE II

(The scene opens with Alapini in the home of Awokoya, an Oyo priest lamenting)

ALAPINI: Awokoya, I am finished. I am done for!

AWOKOYA: What is your problem? Did your wife die or did you lose your manhood?

ALAPINI: Haba! None of the above, but...

AWOKOYA: So why are you jumping up and down like a dog in heat? Calm down, man and tell me the reason for this agitation.

ALAPINI: The cat is out of the bag, Awo.

AWOKOYA: Meaning?

ALAPINI: Queen Olu's daughter, Olobun, the one we hired assassins to kill has been found. She is in the palace as we speak.

(Awokoya rushes to cover Alapini's mouth. He casts a furtive look around to ensure no one is around to hear Alapini)

AWOKOYA: Ogbeni big mouth, how is that possible? We instructed them to kill the other twin, too.

ALAPINI: Apparently, they didn't. And now, the rest of the cut snake is rearing its head to exact revenge.

AWOKOYA: What do you mean by revenge? We did nothing wrong as far as I'm concerned. The children were an abomination and could not be allowed to live.

ALAPINI: I think we made a mistake interfering. Since Alaafin had gone soft because of the witch, Olu, we should have taken it in stride and allowed Obatala, the creator god, to exact his revenge on the royal household.

AWOKOYA: Oh oh! Now I see your true colour. At the first sign of trouble, you grab your breasts like a woman and flee. Real men take the hard decisions and do what needs to be done. You are no man, Alapini. You are just a weakling with a snake between his legs.

ALAPINI: Awo, don't even go there. Weren't you also shaking like a leaf when I told you Olobun was back?

AWOKOYA: Me! *Ajanaku to n ranse p'ogun, ti n ba tun d'oju ogun, ma f'awon ya peerere bi agbado oojo, l'ogun ba tan* (I, the elephant that sends for war, when I arrive the battlefield, I tear them all apart like day fresh maize, and the battle ends). Alapini, how dare you imply that I, Awokoya, was afraid? I was only trying to help you calm down.

ALAPINI: Have you finished with your theatrics so we can get on with the matter at hand? What do we do? If Alaafin digs deep enough, he'll find our hands all over it.

AWOKOYA: There is nothing for him to find. No one can identify us. The stupid guards were asleep when we murdered the boy and we didn't go after the rest of the party ourselves. We came back to Oyo to get mercenaries who were well-paid. So, Alapini, I'm sure we have nothing to worry about.

ALAPINI: A foretold war does not kill the wise cripple. Let us join heads and find a solution.

AWOKOYA: I have no intentions of joining my head with that coconut you call a head.

ALAPINI: Instead of you to let us find a lasting solution to our problem, you are acting like a cocky peacock.

AWOKOYA: Eh! You know what? It is getting late. Come and start going home.

ALAPINI: But we have not finished our discussion. I have been here three times since the girl's return, and this is the first time I'm meeting you. Now you are asking me to leave. I will go nowhere until we find a solution like real men.

AWOKOYA: Real men abi? Awodele, Abiara! *(Two young men run in)* Escort Alapini out of my house.

ABIARA: *Karaole o*! Baba, it is time to leave.

ALAPINI: Do you realise I am a legitimate chief of Oyo and no one has any right to order me?

(Silently, Awodele stoops, lifts Alapini bodily, and carts him off.)

ALAPINI: Awokoya, your protégés are throwing me out of your house! Awodele, are you insane? Put me down this instance! Awokoya, you will regret this! *(Exits)*

AWOKOYA: Imagine the fool insulting me in my own house.

(Alapini runs back in with a shaky voice)

ALAPINI: Awokoya, please pity your good friend. Kabiyesi has called a meeting tomorrow and I must attend. Please tell me what to do.

AWOKOYA: Awodele, Abiara, take him out! This time around, ensure that he stays out.

(Alapini struggles with the young men, but eventually, he is unceremoniously bundled off.)

SCENE III

(Alaafin is seen soliloquising)

ALAAFIN: Olobun's return has brought me so much peace. My heart is light and my joy knows no bounds. Ah! Olu, I wish you were here to see your daughter; she looks so much like you. Her gentle gait settles the palace folks. Peace like never before has settled over the home of my fathers. She is truly a blessing.

(Iyaloja comes in and catches the last of Alaafin's words)

IYALOJA: That she is, a true blessing.
ALAAFIN: Iyaloja, I didn't hear you come in.

IYALOJA: Kabiyesi ooo! That's because you were caught up in your musings.
ALAAFIN: What news from Alapini? What did he have to say for himself?

IYALOJA: Kabiyesi, Alapini begs that he does not wish to return to the palace until the wraith is cast out.

ALAAFIN: What! Does he still insist that Olobun is Olu reincarnated?

IYALOJA: I'm afraid so Kabiyesi.

ALAAFIN: Then he is indeed a fool. Now that she is here, I realise that she is a delight to be with, and the times I spend with her give new meaning to the reason for her existence.

IYALOJA: But Kabiyesi, something bothers me. I have a feeling there is more to this than meets the eye.

ALAAFIN: After hearing Olobun's story, I know something is not right. There is a bit of the puzzle still missing. *(Calls a guard)* Go now and inform all the chiefs to convene here in two days. Tell Alapini particularly that he will feel the weight of my hand should he not attend my summons.

(Guard exits)

SCENE IV

(Iyun, now Olobun, walks in and notices Alaafin in a pensive mood.)

IYUN: Kabiyesi, what's the matter? You look troubled. I thought it was not befitting for a king to look worried. It would affect his subjects.

ALAAFIN: *(Smiling)* And who told you this?

IYUN: Baba Oranyan, of course.

ALAAFIN: *(Laughing)* Next time you see Baba, please tell him he should let me instruct my daughter myself. After all, no one assisted him with his children.

IYUN: *(Laughing)* I have heard you, Kabiyesi. So, what is really bothering you?

ALAAFIN: The same issue that has plagued my mind since you showed up. For one, the ambush in which your brother was killed appears to have been well planned. They had too much information. A stranger cannot arrive in town at night and point out where our grandmother was buried in the afternoon without the interference of an insider. Something is not right. I believe you and your twin brother were the target of that attack at Epe.

(Sitting) Ija told me that immediately your mother saw them butcher your brother, she raised the alarm and it was then they started to scramble around for valuables. This leads me to believe that they were assassins disguised as robbers. They must have been sent by someone within my council who was privy to my decision to let you live in exile.

IYUN: But father, is there anyone in your cabinet you feel is capable of betraying you?

ALAAFIN: Well, no. But from all indications, there's just one person who stands to gain if you die and the kingdom willed to you at birth is left with no monarch – Obade. Just before your return, I was ready to give your kingdom to Obade.

IYUN: But Prince Obade never knew that you would eventually give him my kingdom.

ALAAFIN: Yes. But it is tradition that a kingdom without a monarch is passed on to royal kin. Presently, Obade is the next prince in line to be given a kingdom should any be available. Oyo has not conquered any new lands in years, so he has been deprived of that.

IYUN: That is not a confirmation of treachery, Kabiyesi. 17 years ago, Obade must have been too young to plot anything of the sort. It's either he has an over-ambitious godfather, or he was born to parents who are evil geniuses.

(Iyaloja comes in but is unnoticed by the discussants.)

ALAAFIN: Or maybe it was not just your kingdom the assassins were after.

IYALOJA: Kabiyesi oo. *(She kneels)* Olobun.

IYUN & ALAAFIN: Iyaloja.

IYALOJA: Kabiyesi, I think we are looking for the wrong thing in the wrong place.

ALAAFIN: How do you mean, Iyaloja?

IYALOJA: Killing the twins does not ensure their kingdom would be taken away. Olu could have remained alive to bear you another child, one way or another. I think the reason the twins were targeted is that someone felt it was wrong that they were spared.

ALAAFIN: That makes a lot more sense, Iyaloja. This was more righteous indignation than cold calculation.

IYUN: Kabiyesi, I agree. We need to flush out the culprit.

ALAAFIN: If there's one thing I'm sure about, it is that someone who has killed before for personal belief will do so again, especially when given a reason and the opportunity to. This is what we will do.

(Blackout)

SCENE V

(Iyun can be seen lounging on a mat in the palace yard seemingly alone. She appears to be asleep.)

ALAPINI: *Ago onile o!* Good afternoon, palace inhabitants. Where has everyone gone to? *(Alapini enters and sees Iyun sleeping. He thinks quickly then obviously comes to a decision)* Ehn! This is a perfect opportunity I must not miss. A rare chance to finish what we started *(He approaches the prone Iyun with arms outstretched in a strangling motion. Just as he is about to strangle her, Ija and Abeo spring out of hiding.)*

IJA: Ah ah! You are done for. So, you are part of the perpetrators Kabiyesi was talking about. You ...

ABEO: Ija, must you say everything? Why must you run your mouth at every opportunity? Don't you know that there is a code of conduct for every job? As a security man, you shouldn't reveal the details of your mission, especially to apprehended culprits.

IJA: Abeo, you have come again o! Why won't you let me shout now? Do you think it is easy to catch a big fish?

ALAPINI: Fish ke?

IYUN: It seems staying in the forest has dulled both your senses. You are chatting instead of taking the criminal away. Are you waiting till he kills me before you do something?

ALAPINI: My Princess, it is not my fault o. It was Esu!

IYUN: Take him away, please.

(Abeo and Ija bundle the crying Alapini out.)

ACT FIVE

SCENE I

(The palace. Villagers can be seen strolling in twos and threes into the palace grounds. Alaafin comes out of his chambers flanked by his wives, his many children, and chiefs. Iyun can also be seen sitting with the other children alongside her parents. Alaafin starts to talk.)

ALAAFIN: People of Oyo, my heart is bursting with joy that I will witness this day in my reign. First, my daughter, Olobun, has returned to the ancestral home of her fathers. Secondly, the tradition of killing twins at birth is abolished. No longer will Oyo spill the blood of its own children. Instead, we will use the blood of our enemies to cleanse our land. *(The crowd cheers wildly till Samu calms them down)*

Before I go on, some people need to tell us their stories. Please listen attentively so that when judgment is passed, no one will say the culprits were treated unfairly. Esho Ikoyi, bring in Alapini and Awokoya.

(Two guards run out and return with Alapini and Awokoya. Pointing at the duo, Kabiyesi continues his story). Behold the faces of the traitors. As you know, it is our tradition to kill twins at birth to prevent the calamity the taboo of their birth brings. 17 years ago, my favourite Olori, Olu, was delivered of a set of twins and my heart was broken. I knew the children would be executed, so I consulted Ifá on alternative measures.

CROWD: Ha! Kabiyesi! *(Many grumble at the special treatment Alaafin's twins received.)*

ALAAFIN: Yes, I did it. I am a king, the second in command to the gods, so I questioned them in search of an alternative. It was the gods themselves who gave me my alternative.

FLASHBACK

SCENE II

17 years ago

(Palace attendants can be seen running around busily. Two attendants, a man and a woman, are talking excitedly.)

LAWUNMI: Twins! Abomination.

IBIYEMI: What will Alaafin do?

LAWUNMI: To think the fate of twins in Oyo is a very unfortunate one.

IBIYEMI: Not only that, Olori Olu runs the risk of being ostracised or exiled. If I were her, I would run far away from Oyo with the children. Is it easy to give birth to one child, let alone two? You are a man; I wouldn't expect you to understand. May my privates not burn in childbirth for nothing.

(A palace guard who had been listening all along answers her.)

ESHO: It is not only your privates that will burn, your talkative mouth will burn as well. You had better return to your duties before any of the Oloris meets you here or your fate would be worse than that of the twins.

(They all scamper off as Alaafin walks in with his chiefs, Ifá Priest, Tella and Awokoya.)

ALAAFIN: What tragedy! My beloved wife produced twins. Impossible! I who has ordered the execution of many will with the same mouth order the execution of my blood. Children born to me by my *aayo*. Ha! Eledumare. What manner of tribulation is this?

SAMU: Kabiyesi, please take it easy. We all understand your plight.

AWOKOYA: Ehn, Kabiyesi. We know we cannot kill the initiate the same way we will kill a novice, so we will relieve you of the burden of giving the order by helping you give the order.

IYALOJA: What!

AWOKOYA: Yes.

ALAAFIN: Enough! There will be no killing. That is why Tella is here today to ask Ifá what alternative measures can be taken.

ALAPINI: Abomination, Kabiyesi.

AWOKOYA: This is a tradition that has been in place before you were born. You have no right to change it!

SAMU: Alapini, Awokoya, how dare you tell Alaafin what he can and cannot change?

(Kabiyesi rises in anger.)

ALAAFIN: Awokoya, Alapini, is either of you now the Alaafin and I one of your chiefs that you question one of my directives? Has my gentility become the stupidity of men that you now dare to make pronunciations in my presence? You dare to look upon the face of me, Alaafin, *iku baba yeye, alase ekeji orisa!* Ha!

ALAPINI & AWOKOYA: *(Prostrating)* We are sorry, Kabiyesi. We spoke out of turn. Please forgive us.

ALAAFIN: Esho Ikoyi! Immediately after this meeting, take these two to the prisons. Let them mingle with the prisoners for three days so that they understand how to properly respect their king.

ESHO: Kabiyesi o!

ALAAFIN: Tella, ask Ifá what I must do to waive this evil that towers over my spirit.

(After lengthy consultations, Tella comes up with an answer.)

TELLA: Ifá says live and let live! *Ifá* speaks. *Ifá* provides an alternative. *Ifá* says we should send the queen and the children far away from here to the land within Oyo's realm where yam stalks grow, East of Oyo.

(Kabiyesi heaves a sigh of relief.)

ALAAFIN: Is that all?

TELLA: *Ifá* adds a clause that I do not understand. But it may have some meaning for you.

SAMU: What is the clause?

TELLA: *Ifá* says '...if they will be allowed to live'.

ALAAFIN: What does that mean? This is no time for riddles, man. Out with it.

TELLA: I do not know Kabiyesi. If I did, I'd tell you.

SAMU: Kabiyesi, why not let us begin preparations for the twins to leave? We can worry about that later.

AGBAAKIN: But Kabiyesi, don't you think it will spell doom for Oyo if the twins...?

ALAAFIN: Let no one speak of this matter again. *(He rises)* They leave tonight.

(Kabiyesi walks out as the chiefs genuflect.)

BASHORUN: Abomination! Kabiyesi takes such a decision without consulting me! Who will he call on when the shadow of enemy forces falls on Oyo's gates? Who? These abominable children that Alaafin wants to spare over his whimsical feelings for a woman will be the doom of Oyo.

AWOKOYA: *Okunrin mewa*, why did you say nothing in the presence of Kabiyesi? Oh, your tongue was under siege then. You had better keep your mouth shut. Kabiyesi has made his decision. Those who do not like it should come with me so we can appease the gods and set things right.

ESHO: Baba, it is time to go to prison.

AWOKOYA: My son, but we all know Alaafin was only kidding now. *(Laughs)* You children of nowadays take everything too seriously. Come and see me in the evening, I will send something to you and your colleagues.

ESHO: Baba Awokoya, I will come and see you in three days after your release from prison. Now, please you and Alapini need to come with me before I order the men to carry you.

ALAPINI: Are you joking? Please be joking.

ESHO: No, I am not. Alaafin gave a direct order. You can send people to appeal to him. But until he says so, you are going with me to prison.

(The erring chiefs try to protest. The palace guards manage to suppress them as the other chiefs plead for the gentle handling of their colleagues. Tella sneaks out while the ruckus persists.)

SCENE III

(Alaafin is seen in Olu's chambers with Olu and the babies.)

ALAAFIN: Arrangements have been made for you to leave tonight.

OLU: My lord, I understand the number of laws you must be breaking for me.

ALAAFIN: I am the law.

OLU: But Alaafin, need we go through all this? When I think of all the mothers who have given birth to twins like me, whose hands presently lay bare, I feel our actions betray their sacrifice. I feel like I am betraying motherhood by not sacrificing my children. Will it be fair that Alaafin who gives the orders for twins to be executed goes soft at the sight of his own children?

ALAAFIN: Do not question me, woman, or I'll strangle the babies myself!

OLU: Then do so Kabiyesi and save yourself from the shame this decision brings. But don't forget to kill me in the process.

(She bursts into tears and Alaafin comforts her.)

ALAAFIN: We are mere clay in the hands of the potter. Eledumare alone knows why this is happening.

OLU: I have this unsettling feeling that I will never see Oyo again.

ALAAFIN: You will, Olu. The moment the children are old enough, you may return to Oyo. But for now, go with them. They need you.

(Lights go out.)

SCENE IV

(It's dusk and Olu is seen with a large retinue leaving the palace. Alaafin and Olu sneak last-minute words and seek solace in each other's embrace.)

ALAAFIN: Take care of Olobun and Oluade.

OLU: I will, Kabiyesi. One day, our descendants will walk this very soil we stand on, and they will be called blessed.

ALAAFIN: And you, my dearest queen, the rarest of all my gems, my eyes will behold your beauty that captured my heart again. Go with Eledumare, my brave queen.

(They embrace and move in opposite directions.)

SCENE V

(Alapini and Awokoya have just been released from prison. As they walk, they plot)

AWOKOYA: Imagine. Just because of that witch, Olu, Alaafin put us in jail.

ALAPINI: At least, you are used to jail. It is no strange place to you. Imagine me, a prestigious chief of Oyo rubbing shoulders with all kinds of criminals like a commoner. Ha! I have suffered.

AWOKOYA: Well done o, Oyo chief prisoner. Please leave your stupid ego aside and let us figure out how to do Alaafin's job for him.

ALAPINI: Wait o. Which job?

AWOKOYA: Killing the twins, of course! It has been three days. We need to find out where they are and kill them.

ALAPINI: Ha! That will no longer be for the ritual. That will be murder!

AWOKOYA: Okay. It means your three days in jail taught you nothing. Go to your house and let us forget about it.

ALAPINI: But won't you do something? If we allow Alaafin to get away with this, then we have failed the gods and our suffering will be in vain.

AWOKOYA: Oh! Now, I understand you. You want me to be the one to do something while you rest in the comfort of your home. You are wicked.

ALAPINI: Okay. What should we do? I know the gods will protect us because we are working for them.

AWOKOYA: Exactly! This is what we will do. We will leave Oyo without getting home. After all, no one knows we have been released yet.

ALAPINI: But that means we have to move very fast. You know they left three days ago.

AWOKOYA: Yes, but I am sure we will catch them because they would be slowed down by the burden of the children and their mother.

ALAPINI: That's true. Now that we have decided, let us not waste time before someone sees us.

(They exit.)

SCENE VI

(A small encampment. Everyone is asleep as Awokoya and Alapini sneak in. The twins are equally asleep beside their mother. Awokoya, who is closer to the babies, grabs one of them and strangles it. The baby makes a small sound and Olu awakens.)

OLU: Who is there? Help me! Ija! Esho Ikoyi! Help!

(As Ija awakens, Alapini and Awokoya scamper off. They hastily grab random items on their way out. The guards chase them, but they escape all the same with their 'loot'. Olu's cry follows them for a distance.)

ALAPINI: Awokoya, which one of them were you able to kill?

AWOKOYA: *(Breathlessly)* I don't know. I just know one of them died in my hands.

ALAPINI: Should we go back for the other one?

AWOKOYA: Ha! No o. We cannot go back. We have lost the element of surprise.

ALAPINI: Then what do we do? We cannot leave the job half-done.

AWOKOYA: Shut up and let me think. If we go back now we will be caught, so that means we can no longer do it ourselves.

ALAPINI: So, who will do it?

AWOKOYA: We can find mercenaries. I know a few in Oyo that will do it.

SCENE VII

(Olu's encampment. It is a week after the attack and Olori Olu and her retinue have continued on their journey after burying Oluade.)

IJA: Olori, I think we should stop here tonight. We are getting close to the area where Tella directed us. You are tired. No one has really slept since we buried Oluade. I think it is time to stop moving.

OLU: They killed my son. Why? We left Oyo. Why did evil follow us?

(As Olu laments, a group of mercenaries attack them. Ija and the Eshos fight back as Olori Olu tries to run with Olobun.)

MERCENERY: Find me the baby! Kill it if you can.

(Hearing this, Olori Olu places Olobun in a basket laid with a rich aso-oke. She removes all her adornment of costly iyun, places them in the basket with the baby, and hands the basket to her maid, Ajiun.)

OLU: Ajiun, take her and run. Hide her well. If they find her, they will kill her. Run!

AJIUN: Olori, I can't leave you. If Alaafin discovers I left you, he will kill me.

OLU: He will kill you if Olobun dies. Now run!

(Ajiun picks up the basket and flees, but not before two of the mercenaries sight her. As they try to chase her, Olori Olu

jumps on the back of one of them and starts to bite him furiously. However, the other follows Ajiun unnoticed.)

(Ajiun stops at the edge of a river, tired and out of breath, and this is where the mercenary meets her. Quickly, she places the basket in the crook of a tree at the edge of the river. As she waits for the mercenary behind another tree, she prays fervently to any listening gods.)

AJIUN: Please save Olobun. Save us. I don't want to die. Please don't let them hear her cry.

(Ajiun's prayers unfortunately distract her from her surroundings, and the mercenary sneaks up on her and kills her. He searches the surroundings for any sign of life and, seeing none throws her body into the river and runs off).

(The wind howls, announcing an impending storm. Olobun's cry rends the air as the river's swell reaches the edge of her tree and carries her with the basket into its body.)

SCENE VIII

(It is an underwater palace filled with beautiful women. Osun lounges on a soft fluid-like surface as her attendants rub camwood on her skin. It's a serene environment until the cry of a baby pierces the atmosphere. At the same time, an attendant rushes in to sepeak with Osun.)

ATTENDANT: Ogun seeks an audience, my lady.

OSUN: Ogun Onire in my domain? *(Laughs)* How interesting. Show him in and leave us.

(As her attendants file out, Ogun swaggers in.)

OSUN: Ogun Onire!

OGUN: Osun.

OSUN: When you hear 'gbi gbi gbi' in the compound of the hunter, you know it is Ogun pounding yams.
Ogun that watches over the home of the hunter while he is away.
Ogun, the raging fire that sweeps the forest.
Ogun whose child you can never reprimand.
The one whose red eyes no one wishes to see.
When he hears of war in the neighbouring village,
He sends emissaries to invite the war to his abode.
In the middle of the battle, he calls his enemies together.

And rips them apart like freshly
harvested maize.
Ogun, he impregnates the woman who
refuses to bear children.

What a delight it is to see you. You have been a stranger for too long.

(Osun hugs Ogun while chuckling in her lilting voice.)

Oh! Ogun, put your arms around me and forget about your manly demeanour for a minute. It has been far too long!

OGUN: Osun! Osun sengese,
Always shinning like a golden vessel
Osun, my lady with the undersea palace
The one who grants favours without
redeeming pledges
What have you put in your waters that it
breathes life?
Yeye omo eja olomi iye.
Osun, when I call you, hear me
Osun, do not ignore my supplication.

I greet you my lady. Your words are music to my ears. You know me too well. How have you been?

OSUN: Oh, I've been well. I missed you at the last two councils of the gods. Why must you maintain this solitude you like so much? You should come out and play once in a while, you know?

(The sound of a baby crying rends the air again just before Ogun can respond.)

OSUN: I am so sorry about the noise. I'll send my attendants to investigate and put an end to it.

OGUN: But that is why I am here Osun, that baby crying.

OSUN: Really? You want me to take the child? Is it a girl?

OGUN: No. I want you to simply care for the child till she is found. And yes, the child is a girl.

OSUN: You know I will do anything for you, Ogun. But you must tell me why this girl is so special afterward. I never knew a child could be special enough for you to come out of solitude and visit my palace. That is so out of character for you.

(Osun signals her attendants and whispers to them. They move out briskly.)

OGUN: Thank you for this kindness, Osun. I won't forget it.

OSUN: Come off it, Ogun. You know I do not require thanks when it comes to the protection of children. Now, tell me the fascinating story of this child that has brought you to me for the night.

OGUN: For the night?

OSUN: Yes, for the night. You didn't think I would let you go so easily, did you? I haven't seen you in ages. Besides, if you didn't want to stay, why did you come here looking so good? Here you are in your battle regalia, yet there is no battle in sight. Of course, it means the battle will be in my chambers tonight.

(Osun laughs as Ogun is infected by her laughter and joins in).

So, before we retire, tell me who this child is.

OGUN: Her name is Olobun. She will grow to become Oba Pupupu. She is the daughter of the Alaafin of Oyo, and she will be the mother of a new generation of my people.

OSUN: Isn't that a big burden to place on such a young child?

OGUN: She won't be young forever; she will grow into whatever her people need her to be. But one thing is certain: she will be the matriarch of a new people. Olobun is already a child of legacy. At birth, she created a legacy, and I know that it is not the end of her journey, especially since she has survived despite destiny's curveballs.

OSUN: What curveballs?

OGUN: She was born a twin. That is a death sentence in Oyo, but she survived. When *Ifá* provided an alternative, misguided people came after her, but she survived again. Who would have thought she would be the one to live instead of her brother? She still survived another assassination attempt tonight. It is high time I stepped in. Her blood has become sacred. She will not die by the blade. She will live to grow old.

OSUN: That is truly impressive. I do not understand why you are shocked at this though. Women were created to do more than bear children.

OGUN: Yes, I do know that.

OSUN: Do you? It seems all you gods forget it, and you need to be reminded from time to time. Remember Moremi Ajasoro. Remember my own story.

OGUN: What is your point in all this, Osun? I grow tired of long unending discussions; I am a man of action.

OSUN: Calm yourself, Ogun, and I will get to it. The truth is that men forget that women are a deliberate creation. That is why the strength of a woman goes beyond her ability to bear pain in silence; it is her ability to evolve into who is needed at every point in history: a warrior, a mother, a friend, a lover, a healer, a leader or even a monarch. In the end, she becomes stronger and unafraid to fight for her happiness. But must she suffer to become all of this?

OGUN: I see you are getting passionate. It is a matter for another day. Let us focus on rescuing Olobun. I am sure that as man evolves, so will his understanding.

OSUN: I hope so.

(Osun's attendants walk in and whisper into her ears. After they leave, she faces Ogun)

Olobun has been rescued. She was transported to the other side of the river and placed in the path of a barren woman. If the woman picks her up, merely touching the water on the basket would heal her and open her womb. But she has to choose to pick the child. Fertility would be her reward for rescuing your matriarch.

OGUN: Thank you, Osun. You have been a gem.

OSUN: My pleasure as always. Now, let's go in, so I can help you take off your battle regalia.

(Ogun laughs as he follows her in. Lights out.)

The Present

Scene IX

(The crowd is visibly angry after hearing Alapini and Awokoya's part in the treachery against Olobun. Fola and Aduke equally share their story and Alaafin passes judgment.)

ALAAFIN: Not only did these fools collude with unscrupulous elements, but their actions could have brought about the fall of Oyo.

Alapini, because you are a chief of Oyo, you cannot simply be killed. Esho Ikoyi, present Alapini with his calabash.

ALAPINI: No! Kabiyesi, I beg you! Don't let them give me the calabash! Exile me instead. Please. Awokoya pushed me into this. He was the one who told me we were working for the gods.

ALAAFIN: Then you are in luck. Since you were working for the gods, pick one of them to sacrifice yourself to so that you can complete your service, idiot. I curse you, Oyo curses you, and the gods turn their backs to you.

(Alapini is dragged away as he screams and begs.)

Awokoya. You have supervised and carried out many killings in Oyo in your chosen role as executioner. For betraying your king, and your part in the killing of a prince of Oyo, you will be sacrificed to Ogun. Your generation will never hold any position of value again in Oyo.

AWOKOYA: This cannot be true. I am a messenger of the gods. How can I be killed? No, it is not possible!

ALAAFIN: Take him away. In his next life, he will understand what it means to be a messenger of the gods.

(Awokoya is dragged out of Alaafin's presence as he protests.)

AWOKOYA: Alaafin, don't do this. The gods will be angry with you. I carried out their mission. Oyo will pay if you kill me.

ALAAFIN: Folaranmi, Aduke, for taking my daughter into your home and raising her with love, I give you the freedom to choose where you would live. Wherever you choose you will be given lands and valuables, including ten strong slaves and your name would be known all over Oyo as friends of Alaafin.

FOLA & ADUKE: Alaafin, we are grateful. We choose to go wherever Olobun goes.

ALAAFIN: So be it then. Olobun, please come forward. *(She steps close to her father.)* As much as I wish to have you with me in my palace, it would be a betrayal to all of the twin children whose lives were taken before your time. For this reason, your destiny is no longer in Oyo. Your journey is just beginning as I am sure you have realised. You will build your own kingdom, independent of Oyo but forever linked, and it will be a great one. To ensure that your right to the monarchy is never questioned, I give you a beaded crown that you will pass on to your children.

Your legacy in Oyo is that your birth ended the killing of twins. But your legacy outside Oyo will be that of a matriarch who survived despite the odds and the gods. May Eledumare see you through.

CROWD: Ase!

OLOBUN: *(Kneeling and bowing, she speaks)* Thank you, Alaafin. I will build a kingdom that will make you proud. My people will be known for the strength of their character. Our language will be one filled with passion. We will celebrate life and prosperity, and the pursuit of knowledge will be our waking mantra.

ALAAFIN: Make merry, Oyo, for we have triumphed again! Our empire will be stronger as the new kingdom grows, and Oyo's strength will not wane in my time.

(The crowd cheers as the people dance, sing and make merry.)

THE END

is proud to share a
Monologue on Breast
Cancer

by

Tomi Falade

MY WOMANNESS IS THREATENED!

I'm beautiful.

Don't you just love the way I look, the way I smell, the way I move?

I am a woman; the perfected man – beautiful, graceful, and elegant.

My womanhood is never something to be mocked, never has it been scorned,

because I embody beauty such that your imagination cannot fully comprehend.

You like me the way I am, don't you?

Okay, let's be truthful here; you don't just like it, you love it.

That's because with me you feel good. I make you feel good.

Husband, you flatter yourself with me, my looks, my brains, and most importantly.

my womanness.

2

Oh! Don't get me wrong, I love the fact that you love me. I love the fact that with a careless flick of my tongue I can melt your hardened self.

My womanly parts keep you tied to me even when I'm not there.

You strive daily for it, walking, working, struggling, and yearning to possess it; if not mine, then one of my sex.

To conquer my heart and possess my womanness, you promised me heaven and earth; love so real and protection so secure.

Husband! Now I need you.

My womanness is threatened! Save it.

3

That doctor recommends a double mastectomy to prevent the cancerous cancer that might one day grow in my bosom.

But how do I explain to him that my breasts are the glory of my womanness.

Supple, soft and silky, their tips elevate for my babies – you included husband.

Won't you miss it?

Tell me the truth. Will I be woman enough for you without my twin peaks?

No! Your eyes tell it all even though your tongue says a different thing.

Would I save my life today for an ascetic life, one without the pleasures of the flesh?

I think not. I can't. I won't. I refuse to lose my womanness.

Husband! My womanness is threatened!

4

If you cannot save it, then help me preserve it for as long as it can last.

Let the world shame us for choosing vanity.

Vanity after all is a woman's vice.

Come husband, be my lover tonight and leave the future to the doctor.

If I die tomorrow, I die a woman.

But today, I choose to live whole and complete with my breasts; without fear of the pains of tomorrow – a tomorrow no one can guarantee.

Onaolatomirin Falade *(Dec. 2015)*

A Monologue on breast cancer.

INDEX

I

O

www.ingramcontent.com/pod-product-compliance
Lightning Source LLC
LaVergne TN
LVHW091121150826

845673LV00002B/920

* 9 7 8 9 7 8 7 8 7 2 1 4 7 *